Schismogenesis:

Humor Therapy for Couples in Conflict

"Hey, quit pushing my buttons!"

Erik Douglas Johnson

By the author

A Tyranny of Vapors
Anna the Banana Tree
Another Drink
Ecclesiastes U, Book 1
Ecclesiastes U, Book 2
Ecclesiastes U, Book 3
Ecclesiastes U, Book 4 (work in progress)
Ecclesiastes U, Book 5 (work in progress)
Ecclesiastes U, Book 6 (work in progress)
Either Or, Vol. 1
Either Or, Vol. 2
Faces of Uncertainty, Book 1
Faces of Uncertainty, Book 2
Faces of Uncertainty, Book 3
In Plain View
Invasion of the Marriage Snatcher
Stay Calm When Angry
The Quantum Couple
Yikes!
You vs. You

www.erikdouglasjohnson.com

Dedicated to:

All the good-hearted
and hard-working
therapists, mediators,
pastoral counselors,
coaches, marriage mentors,
social workers, psychologists,
people helpers, and psychiatrists
of Whatcom County, WA.

ISBN-13:978-1985798915
ISBN-10:1985798913

Published by
St. Whimsy Publications
1780 Harksell Road
Ferndale, WA 98248
www.ErikDouglasJohnson.com

Preface to the 2006 Edition

During my twenty years as a mental health professional I was driven, no, obsessed, no, **addicted** to finding the magic bullet that would end couple conflict.

In my role as a family conflict mediator I coached couples on how to argue less and harmonize more by teaching peacemaking skills—responsibility, negotiation, active listening, assertiveness, appreciation, affirmations, compromise, meeting needs, self control, anger management, cognitive therapy, reframing, responding and not reacting, validation and empathy, separating impact from intent, overcoming blame and defensiveness, asking and granting forgiveness, meditation, and more. But guess what?

Couples still argued.

Surely, I thought, there's got to be some intervention, some gadget, some magic formula that ends marital conflict every time. I mean, wouldn't it be cool to invent a therapeutic technique that cures conflict like penicillin kills bacteria?

My wife thought I might be setting my sights too high. *"There's no such thing as a magic bullet that eradicates all domestic quarrels,"* she says. I don't know, maybe she was right. I didn't want to argue.

Nevertheless, my quest continued.

Have you ever been to a theme park or county fair and seen artists draw speedy cartoon likenesses of people's faces? Those drawings are called caricatures and that's what I used to do for fun—simplify and exaggerate the relationships between facial features resulting in—hopefully—an instantly recognizable humorous likeness.

(Incidentally, I've often been tempted to create a business card which on one side said, *"Bored? See Erik the caricaturist"* and on the other side, *"Poor self image due to your caricature? See Erik the therapist."* Anyway….)

Once while drawing at one of these events an idea occurred to me.

What if I simplified and exaggerated the features of marital discord in cartoon form? By pushing to extreme a couples' dysfunctional communication patterns we will create instantly recognizable, humorous, likenesses of the negative traits that contribute to unhealthy fights.

Since therapy consists of bringing into consciousness what we do unconsciously, this collection of caricatured conflicts hopefully will help couples visualize their contribution to marital discord. And, once recognized, eliminate them.

This collection of cartoons is my latest contribution to the field of marriage and family therapy. Whether or not *humor therapy* will be endorsed by the **American Psychological Association** as a surefire magic bullet to end domestic disharmony remains to be seen.

Until then, the peace-making addict that I am, awaits my next fix, good reports of increased couple harmony.

Some words about gender….

Because effective communication styles depend more on emotional intelligence than gender, and because both men and women can behave with maturity and immaturity, I've evenly distributed the number of gaffs between them. Each cartoon could have easily been drawn with male **or** female protagonists. No gender stereotyping is implied or intended.

Erik Johnson
Bellingham, WA 2006

Forward to the 2006 Edition

Schismogenesis (**SKIZZ**-mo-JENNY-sis). The word just rolls off your tongue, doesn't it?

I wish I could take credit for this dandy word but authorship rests instead with a political and social theorist, Gregory Bateson (1904—1980). He coined it in the 1930s to describe how international conflict escalates between nations. Marital therapists, conflict mediators, and dispute negotiators have borrowed the word **Schismogenesis** to help disputants understand the role individuals play in conflict.

"Schismo" refers to division after a dispute. **"Genesis"** means beginning. Put 'em together and you've got a word that means more than merely, "the beginning of division." **Schismogenesis** refers to the process where each disputant may—unwittingly of course—contribute to escalating conflict.

Psychologist Mark E. DeVries tells a story of **Schismogenesis**. His parents got new dual control electric blanket and his over-heated dad kept turning his dial down while his chilly mom kept turning her dial up. Dad got warmer so he dialed down even more. Mom got chillier so she dialed hers up even more. Turns out they got their controls switched! Each one's action triggered a counter reaction from the other.

Communication expert Deborah Tannen , in her book, **That's Not What I Meant** (Ballentine Books, 1986, page 125**)** defines **Schismogenesis** as, "*a mutually aggravating spiral by which each person's response to the other's behavior provokes more exaggerated forms of the divergent behavior.*"

In session with clients I frequently repeat a story I heard on the radio (This American Life, "The Allure of Mean Friends, broadcast August 27, 2004) about a study done in restaurants. Researchers evaluated the impact a waiter or waitresses' friendliness has on customers. It's not hard to imagine the results: the better the service, the bigger the tip. The ruder the service, the smaller the tip. **Schismogenesis** at work.

Once a plant manager said, "I'm going to fire one employee every day until morale improves." He created his own chaos!

Here's another mutually aggravating spiral.

In 1888 Vincent Van Gogh was beside himself with worry that Paul Gauguin was losing interest in the art studio they'd dreamed for years of starting together. For several months they lived and painted together in Southern France and Van Gogh, suspicious about Gauguin's feared departure, constantly hovered over Gauguin, even checking to see if he was in bed at night. Van Gogh made himself a nuisance and the more he fretted the more irritated Gauguin became. The more irritated Gauguin became the more Van Gogh pressured him to stay.

When Gauguin finally did mention leaving, Van Gogh panicked. He tried one last attempt to woo Gauguin to stay—he cut off his ear. Not surprisingly, this strategy didn't work. Gauguin left for Paris immediately. Thus Van Gogh precipitated the very thing he feared most (**Van Gogh, His Life and His Art** by David Sweetman, 286-295).

Thankfully few marriage counselors have to deal with severed ears. But they often deal with **Schismogenesis**.

One partner engages in "perfectly sensible" behaviors thought to woo the other into closeness when in fact those behaviors have the opposite effect.

Frustrations escalate and a vicious cycle ensues. Conflict is exacerbated and the result is "co-created chaos." As we say in counseling, *"When wooing efforts fail to woo, See the other's point of view."*

The good news is that it only takes one party to disengage from **Schismogenesis.** The bad news is that recognizing our role in the chaos is hard. It's so easy to be defensive and blame others for their disappointing actions when in fact their actions are often reactions to our own actions. And our actions are in reality reactions to their earlier actions.

Who starts our couple conflicts? Like the chicken and the egg, we're not sure. But we do know who can end it...the disputant who sees their role in the co-created chaos first and is willing to change it.

Schismogenesis: Humor Therapy For Couples in Conflict will help us see our role in relationship conflict.

If this compendium of negative traits in a marriage seems too negative, ask yourself if you'd like to go to a doctor who never studied sickness. Like the home remedy books that describe pathologies in great detail (and often with sobering color photographs), this book describes (with humor) the pathologies inherent in relational conflict. By familiarizing yourself with these "diseases" couples face we'll know the symptom when we see it.

As an added challenge, ask your partner to read this book and find examples of when and where you may have been guilty of negative communication patterns. We do *not* advise you to find examples of what your partner does to bug you in order to get them to change. Doing so will only set in motion your own **Schismogenesis** and our purpose is to reduce, not generate, division.

Thanks for letting me help you achieve the type of relationship you desire.

Erik Johnson
Bellingham, WA 2006

Forward to the 2018 Edition

Upon my retirement in 2018 I gave myself the task of updating my printed materials and thus continue my peace-making passion, albeit, from afar.

While the word "schismogenesis" is not yet a household word (my efforts notwithstanding), the wily principles of schismogenesis are still hard at work complicating couples' lives and marriages. And the solutions are sound as ever: no more reacting when your buttons are pushed, and do your best not to push your partner's buttons.

My goal in retirement is to squeeze one more career in before I turn 90 (I've got 24 years to go), that of artist/writer. This grand plan includes creating YouTube videos, educational posters, graphic novels, humor pieces, and more, all in the service of promoting harmony between couples, families, and in society at large.

You can follow my work at my new blog: www.erikdouglasjohnson.com.

As of this writing my old website is still up and running, although mostly inactive: www.conflictmediationcoach.com.

"Peace on earth good will toward all."

Erik Douglas Johnson
Ferndale, WA 98248
2018

Schismogenesis:

Humor Therapy for Couples in Conflict

10 Look at your dating partner through a magnifying glass; look at your mate through the opposite end of a telescope. The sooner you learn how your behavior affects your partner, and how your partner affects you, the better.

11 Why is it so hard to see our contribution to conflict? The 21st century is, *"The Age of Uncertainty."* But one thing is certain: making your partner 100% responsible for disputes is a surefire recipe for disaster. Break the denial habit.

12   Psychologists call it, "*instrumental drama.*" As unpleasant as drama can be, the payoff is often worth the hassle. If there's drama in a relationship let's make sure it's not your drama. Learn to love peace and quiet.

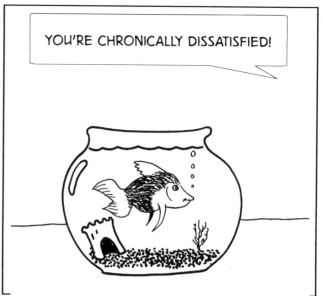

13 As important as meeting each other's needs is, it's not the cure-all many assume. Satisfaction in life requires more than one spouse can provide. And we do not advocate multiple spouses. The abundant life includes tapping other resources.

© 2018 Erik Douglas Johnson   Schismogenesis

14   The proverbial "*love test*" seems so logical. How will we know how much our partners love us unless we bait them? Um, how about asking? Better yet, show lots of love yourself and see how they reciprocate. It takes two to be lovers.

15 Where does blaming come from? High fructose corn syrup? The planets? Neurotransmitters? Hormones? We know of no gene that determines blaming. Most likely, most of us could exercise more self control. We are responsible.

16 Nursing hurt feelings has benefits: preferential treatment, others cater to our needs, others focus on not upsetting us, and people don't expect us to function well since we're in pain. Staying hurt seems odd, but the pay offs are tempting!

Immaturity

Maturity

Responsibility

Irresponsibility

Folly

Wisdom

© 2018 Erik Douglas Johnson   Schismogenesis

17   There are two motives in life—pleasing ourselves and pleasing others. There's a time and place for both, and ignoring one leads to a life out of balance. Be mindful of how your decisions affect others. That's a high ideal!

© 2018 Erik Douglas Johnson   Schismogenesis

18   Nagging: the habit of telling someone twice what they've heard once. Like radio static, nagging garbles communication, irritates the listener, and motivates ear plugging. Be direct, clear, assertive, and then let it go.

© 2018 Erik Douglas Johnson   Schismogenesis

19   The pursuit of happiness is an unalienable right. Making others responsible for our happiness is an unfortunate blunder. Blaming others for our unhappiness is as bad as blaming others for our own choices. Happiness is a choice.

20 Juggling connection _and_ individuality is hard. Marriage invites intimacy but if your need for attachment are low and your need for independence is high, clashes are likely. Define with your partner "we" and "I" and how to mesh them.

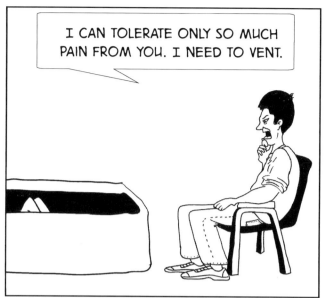

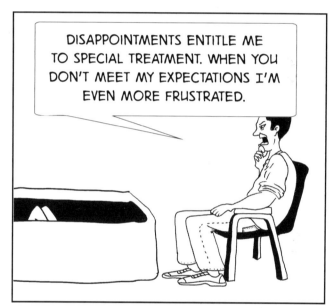

© 2018 Erik Douglas Johnson   Schismogenesis

21   In a partnership both parties have legitimate needs. When those needs clash somebody's got to give. Demanding that your partner sacrifice their needs on your behalf 100% of the time is asking for trouble. Meet your partner's needs.

22 The skill of getting into another person's emotional world is difficult. Feeling what others feel and experiencing what others experience answers the question, "*What must it be like to be in that person's shoes?*" Practice empathy.

23   A marriage between equals is both nurturing and respectful. A husband who needs *"mothering"* is exhausting to his wife. If she's waiting for him to grow up she may wait a long time. To break out of this dependency, stop mothering.

© 2018 Erik Douglas Johnson   Schismogenesis

24 Relationships aren't necessarily damaged by our perceptions, or even by our incorrect perceptions. They're damaged when we refuse to examine our perceptions to see if they're correct or not. It could be that they are wrong. Ouch!

© 2018 Erik Douglas Johnson Schismogenesis

25 Fear of anger can be as problematic as anger itself. Anger avoiders are often conflict avoiders, and avoided conflict won't go away. Anger and conflict happen. Appreciate them like smoke detectors alerting us that something's wrong.

"Guys Who Just Don't Get It"

SHE GETS MAD WHEN I TELL FRIENDS SHE'S "THE CRANKY OLD LADY." YOU NEVER KNOW WHAT WILL SET HER OFF.

WHETHER MORNING OR NIGHT, I NEVER SAY HI TO MY WIFE. I HAVE A GREETING DISORDER.

I WAIT FOR SOMEONE TO TELL ME HOW MY DAY IS GOING. THEN I'LL KNOW HOW TO FEEL ALL DAY.

MY MOTHER, GRANDMOTHER, GIRLFRIENDS, AND EX WIVES ALL KISSED MY OWIES AND MADE 'EM BETTER. WHY DON'T YOU?

UNTIL YOU SPEAK UP AND COMMUNICATE CLEARLY I'M GOING TO IGNORE YOU.

Double standards, cluelessness, neediness, aloofness; the number of ways mates drive each other crazy is astonishing. Happily, getting along isn't a mystery. Like golf or fixing toasters, a few learnable skills make us proficient.

"Gals Who Just Don't Get it"

© 2018 Erik Douglas Johnson   Schismogenesis

27   Do women sometimes not "get it?" To quote Donkey from Shrek 3, "*It wouldn't be inaccurate to assume that I couldn't exactly not say that it is or isn't almost partially incorrect.*" In short, there may be a teensy, weensy chance it's true.

28   It's counter-intuitive, but the more we control the less influence we have. The less we control, the more influence we have. If your attempts at control have backfired try this: relinquish your partner, accept them as is, and see what happens.

29 Communication coaches spend more time teaching "*listening*" skills than "*talking*" skills. Why? The listener has the most influence on the outcome of conversations. If your spouse isn't a good listener, talk less and listen more.

© 2018 Erik Douglas Johnson   Schismogenesis

30 Once a stereotype gets lodged in our head it's hard to dislodge. We discount evidence to the contrary and muster "*proofs*" that confirm our preconceived biases. It's bad enough with strangers, but deadly in a marriage. No labels!

© 2018 Erik Douglas Johnson   Schismogenesis

31   Even the most reasonable among us misread others. We're convinced we always know what others mean or imply. As accurate as intuition can be (even a clock that doesn't run is right twice a day), we're not infallible. No presumption!

32 No problem is so small that it can't be made worse by over-reacting. One of the symptoms of over-reacting is denying being over-reactive! Take a self-quiz: try for one week to respond calmly to every trigger, button pushing, or irritation.

© 2018 Erik Douglas Johnson   Schismogenesis

33 Doing for others what they are unable to do for themselves is an act of kindness. Doing for others what they refuse to do for themselves is called "*enabling bad behavior*." What would happen if you chose to be more responsible?

© 2018 Erik Douglas Johnson   Schismogenesis

34   Giving the silent treatment is so damaging that marriage researcher John Gottman says it's a sign of impending marital disaster. He calls it stonewalling. Communication problems are *not* improved with poor communication.

35   Intimacy has been defined as "*in to me see.*" It's a skill and a gift. By learning how to see into your partner's heart they'll feel connected, validated, and loved. Active listening, empathy, and understanding can be learned. Go for it.

© 2018 Erik Douglas Johnson   Schismogenesis

36   *"A day without faultfinding is like a day without sunshine."* This is the motto of too many people. More astonishing, self-appointed behavior cops rarely see how unpleasant their nasty barbs are. Let's turn nasty jabs into respect.

37   The biological and psychological urge to merge is often so great judgment and powers of discernment fly out the window. The law of large numbers suggests that no matter how risky a relationship might be, there'll be takers.

38 A person who resorts to verbal steamrolling shows that their arguments lack merit. The power to accuse is the power to control. If you want to fight fair, take turns speaking, do not intimidate, go silent, outshout, or strike fear in your partner.

© 2018 Erik Douglas Johnson   Schismogenesis

39 Fear is universal; coping strategies vary. Sadly for spouses of the highly anxious, stabilizing actions sometimes include drama, fights, and provocations. It's better to treat anxiety than to cope by provoking your spouse. Deal with anxiety.

40 If your bed was too short you wouldn't cut off your feet; you'd get a longer bed. If your partner was unhappy with you, you wouldn't get a new partner. You'd get a better attitude, become kind, make adjustments. Marriage means compromise.

WHILE YOU WERE AT WORK TODAY THE KIDS GOT INTO A FIGHT OVER WHO LOST THE TV REMOTE AND I SENT THEM BOTH TO THEIR ROOMS WHICH, BY THE WAY WERE BOTH TOTALLY MESSY AND I WISH YOU'D TALK TO THEM ABOUT PICKING UP THEIR STUFF. IT'S BEEN MONTHS SINCE EITHER OF THEM VACUUMED AND I'M AFRAID IT'S A HEALTH HAZARD WHICH REMINDS ME THAT MY FATHER IS SCHEDULED FOR SURGERY NEXT WEEK AND I'LL NEED TO GET A

REPLACEMENT FOR MYSELF IN THE GYM NURSERY BUT THAT'LL BE HARD BECAUSE .... ARE YOU LISTENING?.... THE CAR IS ACTING UP AND I'D LIKE YOU TO TAKE IT INTO THE SHOP BEFORE I DRIVE TO MY FOLKS' PLACE. I DON'T KNOW WHY MY SISTER CAN'T OFFER TO HELP .... I WISH YOU'D GET MORE EXERCISE AND WHAT'S WITH THAT NEW JAZZ CD? ARE YOU GOING THROUGH A MID LIFE CRISIS? IF YOU'D SPEND

AS MUCH ATTENTION TO ME AS YOU DO TO YOUR STUPID HOBBIES I'D FEEL A LOT MORE SECURE BUT NO, YOU THINK YOU'RE ENTITLED TO PLAY, PLAY, PLAY WHILE I KEEP THIS FAMILY FUNCTIONING AND I'M REALLY GETTING TIRED OF THE LEAKY ROOF WHICH I'VE ASKED YOU TO FIX I DON'T KNOW HOW MANY TIMES. DID YOU CALL THE ROOFER YET? I'M DISSATISFIED WITH THE AMOUNT OF WORK YOU DO AROUND HERE COMPARED TO WHAT OTHER HUSBANDS DO. MARGARET'S HUSBAND NOT ONLY TOOK A COOKING CLASS

WITH HER BUT HE NEVER LETS A HOME REPAIR GO UNFIXED FOR MORE THAN A DAY. SHE'S SO LUCKY. I'VE TRIED TO GET YOU TO CHANGE FOR 20 YEARS BUT YOU JUST DON'T BUDGE. I'M JUST ABOUT AT THE END OF MY ROPE BUT THE KIDS STILL NEED ME AND I KEEP HOPING YOU'LL CHANGE. A TV EVANGELIST IS HAVING A HEALING CRUSADE AND I WISH YOU'D WATCH IT. I JUST KNOW THERE'S SOMETHING WRONG WITH YOU BUT YOU REFUSE TO DO ANYTHING ABOUT IT. I'M ASHAMED WHEN MY GIRL FRIENDS ASK HOW WE'RE DOING

BECAUSE I DON'T WANT TO LIE YET MY FRUSTRATION LEVEL HAS JUST ABOUT BEEN REACHED. YOU NEVER ASK HOW I'M DOING. DON'T YOU CARE? I'M DOUBLY HURT BECAUSE NOT ONLY DO YOU HURT MY FEELINGS BUT YOU DON'T DO ANYTHING TO MAKE ME FEEL BETTER————

DID THE TV REMOTE EVER SHOW UP?

STOP INTERRUPTING! YOU ARE SO CONTROLLING!

41   We have two ears and one mouth so we listen twice as much as we speak, or speak half as much as we listen. Either way, ear fatigue is serious. Partners tune us out when we're too wordy. Cut back on verbiage and see what happens.

42   Some couples bicker not because they're too far apart but because they're too close, without emotional boundaries. One party expects the other to think just like them. Marriage is made of two individuals, not one soul in two bodies.

43 Is it possible to want to be loved too much? Yes. It's difficult for some to grasp, but partners who do no think about us 24/7, who have thoughts that do not include us, who get preoccupied, can still love us. Reduce your need to be needed.

44 The initial brain chemical rush of infatuation, idealization, and the subconscious desire to get from our mate what we didn't get in our family of origin often overrides common sense. Long courtships reveal incompatibilities. Go slow.

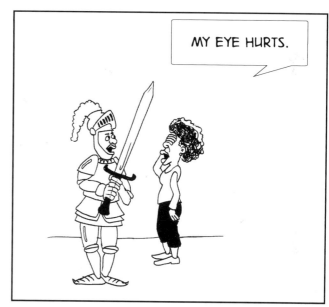

45 The old word, "wooing" should come back into style. It means, "*The art of attracting others into a romantic relationship.*" Wooing begins by identifying those things about us that are not attractive but repellant. Like hurting the ones we love.

"Guys Who Just Don't Get It"

YOU SAY I CONTRIBUTE TO, PROVOKE, INVITE, INDUCE, PRECIPITATE, CUE, PUSH BUTTONS, TEMPT, PROMPT, FUEL, STIMULATE, TRIGGER, CREATE A CLIMATE FOR, AND INSTIGATE YOUR REACTIONS. AT LEAST YOU DIDN'T SAY I CAUSE YOUR FRUSTRATION!

GIVE ME HEAT FIRST THEN I'LL FEED YOU.

GIVE ME RESPECT FIRST THEN I'LL LOVE YOU.

BAD BREATH IS BETTER THAN NO BREATH.

I MUMBLE AND THEN BLAME YOU FOR NOT UNDERSTANDING ME.

© 2018 Erik Douglas Johnson   Schismogenesis

46   Some guys treat their car with more finesse than they do their wife. Love has good manners and it'd be to everyone's advantage for guys to learn to treat their wives as intelligent, worthy, capable, and valuable individuals.

"Gals Who Just Don't Get It"

47 It's the rare individual who tells a counselor their marriage problems are due to their own anxieties. The tendency is to blame, assume a martyr role, and play victim while it's their own insecurities that gum things up. Look in the mirror.

48   Of the many types of anger, instrumental anger is the most insidious. Instrumental anger is anger we practice in order to get something we want. It's calculated, desperate, and the "*instrument*" we use to bludgeon our partners.

© 2018 Erik Douglas Johnson   Schismogenesis

49   Why is it we can recall offenses committed against us in minute detail but are clueless when it comes to offenses we commit? Because selective memory minimizes our role in conflicts and exaggerates others'. Memory self justifies.

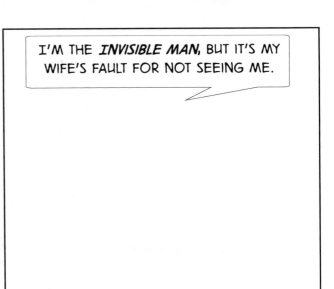

© 2018 Erik Douglas Johnson   Schismogenesis

50   What's worse than contributing to another's pain? Denying it. And what's worse than denial? Saying, "*You're the damaged, hypersensitive, cold-hearted, psychotic one! Any complaints are your doing. I didn't have issues till I met you.*"

© 2018 Erik Douglas Johnson   Schismogenesis

51 What's the payoff for provoking others? When they squawk it gives us something to complain about. When they react it puts the attention on them. When they withdraw it feeds our inner martyr. If they leave it proves we're unlovable.

52 Working for a better relationship is great! Expecting life to confirm to our every whim backfires. Replace expectations with acceptance, resignation, relinquishment, and see what happens. Gratitude rather than griping is good policy.

© 2018 Erik Douglas Johnson   Schismogenesis

53 People with self control, not spouse control, are happy. Explosive, rash, volatile, and unpredictable rants add energy to a relationship but at too high a cost. If you and your spouse don't like escalating fights, learn to calm down!

Schismogenesis

© 2018 Erik Douglas Johnson

54   Carol Tavris says, "*Marriages die the death of a thousand justifications.*" What we excuse, rationalize, or defend may sound reasonable to us, but we don't live with us. Most of us would be shocked to hear our own justifications.

55   Humans have the ability to think and feel; there's trouble if we deny either. Whole persons value logic *and* feelings. Getting our hearts and brains on the same page is powerful. Know what you feel and feel what you know.

© 2018 Erik Douglas Johnson   Schismogenesis

56   While it's true that marriage is a classroom to learn the arts of compromise, communicate, and kindness, men would do well to make it easier on their wives. Deal with PTSD and, "Put the Toilet Seat Down." She'll be very happy.

57   Many emotions are the result of our thoughts, so to control emotions, control your thoughts. This is not an easy task for those prone to ruminate, obsess, and replay old tapes. One strategy: replace troublesome thoughts with good ones.

58   The word "familiar" and "family" come from the same root. The person who felt unloved growing up bristles when shown affection in a new relationship because it feels unfamiliar. Some reenact childhood drama because it's familiar.

59 When we focus on our mate's flaws and our unmet needs, the outcome will be dismal. By working instead on meeting their needs and correcting our flaws we've got influence, integrity, and self control. The outcome is considerably better.

60 People control from fear of unmet needs, fear of the unknown, and fear of vulnerability. To feel safe they manipulate others, control others' choices, and avoid all risk. Ironically, people avoid controllers thus increasing a controller's fears.

© 2018 Erik Douglas Johnson   Schismogenesis

© 2018 Erik Douglas Johnson   Schismogenesis

61 Some people elevate woundedness to a fine art. Rather than taking responsibility to heal, they let their pain fester until everyone learns to treat them with TLC, kindness, and tolerance to avoid the accusation, "*You cold hearted thug!*"

62 How long before we realize it's not others with the problem, but us? Either we're incredibly unlucky, surrounded with liars, false accusers, and "*people with issues*," or we may in fact have some blind spots. Is it them or is it us? Maybe us!

63   Questions for information are wonderful. Questions disguised as snide remarks aren't. Timid folk find it easier to make subtle hints, vague observations, and indirect inquiries rather than coming right out with requests. Too bad.

© 2018 Erik Douglas Johnson   Schismogenesis

64   Desperation isn't attractive. Intimate relationships are a modulated dance of closeness and separateness. Too much separateness equals no relationship. Too much closeness erases individuality. You are not one soul in two bodies.

© 2018 Erik Douglas Johnson   Schismogenesis

65   Trying to hit a moving target is hard. Trying to please a partner who's all over the place is harder. It's helpful when both parties agree on rules for communication. Write them down so you don't forget them in the heat of battle.

66 Cars work best with full gas tanks. Relationships work best with kindness, thoughtfulness, and tenderness. If your engine stalls, fill 'er up. If your marital engine stalls, fill the gas tank of love. A smoother running marriage is worth the effort.

"Gals Who Just Don't Get It"

67 When you met "*the one*." were you expecting unlimited tolerance, super human patience, and tireless efforts to bring you bliss? Sorry, but we know of no such person. You get more of what you need when you flex, negotiate, and "*get*" him.

68   When a marriage is strained it's easy to glom on to a third party for security, which only adds to marital strain if that third party is a step-child or in-law. Don't be surprised, however, if those needy third parties feed the triangulation.

© 2018 Erik Douglas Johnson   Schismogenesis

69 John Gottman's phrase, "*marital poop*," refers to those things in our marriage that, "*just don't smell right*." Let's develop an early warning system that lets you know when your marital quality is in danger. Lower your tolerance for poop.

© 2018 Erik Douglas Johnson   Schismogenesis

70   Many couples have acclimated themselves to so much pain that they stay stuck in marital conflict. Some wait till it's too late to break out of their discomfort, and separate. We suggest you develop an intolerance for pain, and stand up.

Schismogenesis

© 2018 Erik Douglas Johnson

71   Being helpful is a virtue. But if your identity is "*helper*," when your partner is healthy they seem boring. You then wander off and look for other needy people. Or worse, we turn our loved ones into needy souls by hurting them.

© 2018 Erik Douglas Johnson   Schismogenesis

72 Rather than perpetuate the perennial marital quandary of distribution of labor, a little empathy goes a long way. Furthermore, some jobs come easier to some, harder to others, so it's never fair to compare work loads. Work on empathy.

© 2018 Erik Douglas Johnson   Schismogenesis

73 Can a person really be so blind that they're unaware that they bug others? Yup. Self-awareness is a learned skill. Humility is a virtue. Honesty about one's blind spots is a rare gem. How are you triggering your mate's anxiety?

© 2018 Erik Douglas Johnson   Schismogenesis

74   A partner who doesn't "*get it*" may not "*get it*" because the message is confusing. Even an excellent listener can't pick up garbled messages. Privileged white males especially need coaching on the perils facing women.

75   Skin hunger isn't satisfied by mere words, acts of service, or gifts. Sometimes our partner just needs a hug. Withholding physical touch is a serious breach of the marital contract. The vow to "*forsake all others*" means "*cuddle up!*"

© 2018 Erik Douglas Johnson   Schismogenesis

76   Why are some partners stingy with kindness? It's cruel to invite a mate to open up and then punish them for doing so. It not only makes them wary about opening up in the future, it leaves them feeling uncared for. Double whammy!

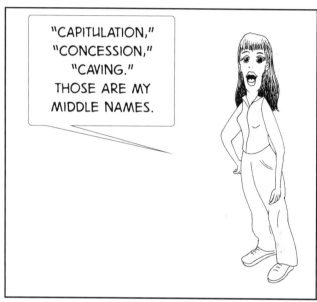

77   One way to measure being tolerant vs. being overly compliant: a lost voice. Every person has a right to safety, opinions, insights, input, values, tastes, _and_ a right to say so. If this right is denied it may be timidity...or abuse.

78 Wanting reassurance that we're loved makes sense. But often "*love tests*" are guaranteed to fail. The motive behind such tests sometime isn't reassurance but an excuse to scold our partner. Instead, set up your partner to succeed.

79   When challenged we call in reinforcements to validate our innocence. Problems occur, however, when those reinforcements are biased, prejudiced, or have incomplete data. What would an impartial jury say about your case?

80   If there was only one gender there'd be no gender gap. But with two genders it's easy to blame communication blunders on the worst stereotype of each other. Best not to label one way or another. Just speak and listen attentively.

81   Communication gaffs between Chinese and Latvian speakers are due to not learning each other's mother tongue. Here's an encouraging fact: men and women have been communicating for millennia. So it can be done. Trust me.

© 2018 Erik Douglas Johnson   Schismogenesis

82   Logic is a tool to find truth, provided with stick to the rules. Sadly, selective thinking makes us notice only what confirms out beliefs while we ignore ideas which contradict our beliefs. Evaluate beliefs about your partner logically.

© 2018 Erik Douglas Johnson   Schismogenesis

83   Therapists love seeing clients turn over a new leaf. They also recognize partners may need time before celebrating. This is especially true if they've heard, *"I've changed!"* many times. Like the boy who cried wolf, building trust takes time.

© 2018 Erik Douglas Johnson   Schismogenesis

84   Some people are so convinced that they know what their partner is thinking they don't believe it when they're wrong. Just because you're right once in a while doesn't mean you're right all of the time. Stay out of your partner's head.

© 2018 Erik Douglas Johnson   Schismogenesis

85   It's true that failure to attach securely in infancy makes it hard (not impossible) to attach as adults. It's hard work but one can learn to trust others and believe that they are indeed lovable. That's the basis of a secure attachment.

86 WARNING: relationships can only carry so much contempt before a fuse is lit and things explode. If you're unhappy with your mate channel your anger into problem-solving and marriage-building. Contempt will blow you both to bits.

87 People averse to boredom stir up conflict for entertainment. Some say a good fight is as energizing as good sex. We're not sure adrenaline addiction is good for your heart, so find a healthy alternative to "*fight*" entertainment.

88 The human psyche is complex. It can want two different things at the same time. What a dilemma! The problem is when we want both honesty *and* immunity from hearing hurtful things. You can't have both at the same time.

89   Some people think any old excuse will get them off the hook, even a bad excuse. They think just giving reasons for their offence is like a "*get out of jail free*" card. We expect kids to think like this. But adults? Yikes!

"Guys Who Just Don't Get It"

WHAT DO YOU MEAN I'M INSENSITIVE? WHEN MY NEEDS ARE UNMET I FEEL IT DEEPLY!

SURE I THREATEN YOU AND THEN MOCK YOU FOR BEING A COWARD. 'ZATTA PROBLEM?

HAVING NEEDS MEANS YOU'RE NEEDY.

"*DIVORCE IS NOT AN OPTION*' MEANS I'M FREE TO MESS UP ALL I WANT AND MY WIFE WON'T TAKE ANY ACTION!

MY NET WORTH DETERMINES MY SELF WORTH.

90   If a truck is too tall to fit under an overpass, either raise the overpass, which is costly, or let air out of the tires lowering the truck's height. Marriage is like that truck. Either change your spouse, which is costly, or change you.

"Gals Who Just Don't Get It"

YOU MUST TAKE MY WORDS AT FACE VALUE BUT LET ME READ SPECIAL MEANING INTO YOUR WORDS, TONE OF VOICE AND FACIAL EXPRESSIONS.

HE THINKS I EXPECT HIM TO READ MY MIND. I WISH HE UNDERSTOOD THAT'S NOT TRUE.

HELL IS BEING SURROUNDED BY DOZENS OF NEEDY PEOPLE CRYING, *"I'M NOT HAPPY."*

I TERRIFY LEAST I FEAR!

YOU CAN **NEVER** EARN MY TRUST BUT KEEP TRYING ANYWAY. GIVING UP PROVES YOU DON'T LOVE ME.

91 One guess at the hardest thing about being a woman (besides being discriminated against, misused, and taken advantage of)? That men don't understand or appreciate what's behind the above comments.

92 If the payoff for staying in the *"feeling wounded zone"* is greater than the payoff for healing, people stay in perpetual victim mode. But if the cost of staying wounded was a $100,000 fine, many would find a way to move forward.

© 2018 Erik Douglas Johnson   Schismogenesis

93 Just because something feels true does not make it true. When we harmonize heart, mind, will, and emotions, we filter life through the grid of reason, feelings, and choices. Develop emotional resiliency with thick skin and keen mind.

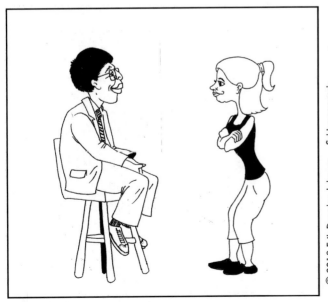

94 The notion "*two become one*" does not mean you meld into one cosmic being without individuality. There are still two individuals in a marriage. Forcing agreement means one of you will disappear. Celebrate and affirm your differences.

95 We put people in impossible situations when we don't respect their choices. Love freely given, and freely withheld, is up to each individual. Coerced love isn't love. Be as loving as possible and if not reciprocated, grieve and move on.

96 A child shouldn't accuse adults of making them feel short. A basketball player shouldn't accuse us of making them feel tall. Likewise, we should not accuse assertive persons of making us feel manipulated. We just may be too timid.

© 2018 Erik Douglas Johnson   Schismogenesis

97   It's obvious, but it's true. Many conflicts could be avoided simply by looking at the person you're talking to. This explains by conversations while driving, on email, or even on the telephone are prone to misunderstanding.

© 2018 Erik Douglas Johnson   Schismogenesis

98 To rationalize is to believe "*rational lies*." And they are lies. Deep down we know we should be nicer, calmer, and less critical. When we balance guilt by making excuses we become childish, disingenuous, and hard to live with.

99 If your date is happy only when they get your adulation, run for the hills. The "*impossible to please*" person won't magically change after the wedding. Proceed only if you like stroking egos, feeding pride, and meeting their every need.

100 It'd be nice if our every need was met without having to ask. Reality demands, however, that we take responsibility for communicating our needs, which requires talking. Don't dump on your partner for not doing what in truth is your job.

© 2018 Erik Douglas Johnson   Schismogenesis

101   If only reading emotions was as easy as reading a text on your phone! If only responding to emotions was as easy as sending texts on your phone! If only couples would spend more time talking ...and less time texting.

102 Whose job is it to make you happy? Yours. If you make it your partner's job to make you happy are you willing to make it your job to make them happy? The happiest couples know how to get happy alone and together.

© 2018 Erik Douglas Johnson   Schismogenesis

103   It's not only what we say to our partners that builds a relationship, but what we say to ourselves. Those who forget to talk to themselves get forgetful. Give yourself frequent stern lectures and grow in self-control.

© 2018 Erik Douglas Johnson   Schismogenesis

104   Marriage is not a grown-up way to play dolls, or train pets. Your partner is a human to be honored. We want marriage to be fun but not at the expense of dignity and propriety. Marriage is a mini-society with big consequences.

105 Most actions in a marriage are actually reactions. It takes two to teeter-totter; and it takes two in a marriage to squabble month after month. If you don't like your actions or reactions, get off the marital teeter-totter.

DEMANDS

UNASSERTIVE

PRESUMPTION

REACTION

LIES

BELITTLING

ANGER

SHAME

STONEWALLING

CONTEMPT

STUBBORNNESS

ACCUSATION

HATRED

ALOOFNESS

WITHDRAWAL

FIGHTS

106   If conflict is a permanent feature of your relationship, if intractable disagreements eat you up, if you argue about the same petty stuff over and over, take up dancing. Is it possible to fight and boogie at the same time? Maybe not.

MY FIRST THREE GIRLFRIENDS WERE CLINGY.

MY FIRST THREE WIVES WERE CLINGY.

MY LAST THREE GIRLFRIENDS WERE CLINGY.

MY CURRANT GIRLFRIEND IS CLINGY.

WHY CAN'T I FIND A WOMAN WILLING TO GIVE WHO...

...DOESN'T EXPECT ANYTHING IN RETURN?

107 If you're interested in a long term relationship—and we believe you are—it's more likely to occur if you're on the giving end of things. Don't be stingy with money, time affection, help, support, knowledge, skills, or friendship.

YOU DRAIN ME DRY THEN CRITICIZE ME FOR BEING EMPTY.

YOU CRITICIZE ME FOR BEING EMPTY AND THEN COMPLAIN THAT I'M DEPRESSED.

YOU COMPLAIN THAT I'M DEPRESSED THEN WHINE THAT I DON'T SNAP OUT OF IT.

YOU WHINE THAT I DON'T SNAP OUT OF IT AND THEN BELLYACHE THAT I WITHDRAW.

YOU BELLYACHE THAT I WITHDRAW AND THEN GRUMBLE THAT I FEEL DRAINED.

YES, I DRAIN, CRITICIZE, COMPLAIN, WHINE, AND BELLYACHE BECAUSE YOU ASKED ME TO GET MORE EXERCISE.

© 2018 Erik Douglas Johnson   Schismogenesis

108 A customer and mechanic can communicate all day but until wrenches get turned the customer isn't happy. A couple can talk about needs all day but until that talk turns to loving action the marriage will suffer. Don't just talk, act!

109   It's often the case that when things get out of hand in a dispute one party will make an attempt to deescalate the fight. Those attempts as "*repair*" can take a variety of forms. Learn to observe them, respect them, and use them.

© 2018 Erik Douglas Johnson   Schismogenesis

110 Good communication isn't measured by how many words both parties speak. It's measured by how effective both parties are at understanding what the other is saying. This requires active listening and asking clarifying questions.

© 2018 Erik Douglas Johnson   Schismogenesis

111 Chronic marital discord suggests that both partners perpetuate fights because both get some need satisfied by chronic conflict. It takes two to tango and two to wrangle. You know your mate's contributions but do you know yours?

OF COURSE I DON'T GIVE MY GIRLFRIEND ANY SLACK.

IF I LENGTHEN THE LEASH SHE'LL GET INTO TROUBLE.

I CONTROL HER FOR HER OWN GOOD.

HER FREEDOM MAKES ME ANXIOUS SO I HOLD THE REINS PRETTY TIGHT.

SHE QUIT FIGHTING ME AND NOW IS MEEK AS A PUPPY.

MY NEXT TRICK WILL BE TO TEACH HER TO FETCH.

112 If you live with a controller you could be part of the problem. How? By putting up with the control. You can't control controllers but you can control your response to control. How will controllers ever stop if you never say, "*NO!*"

© 2018 Erik Douglas Johnson   Schismogenesis

113 It's normal for couples to have differences. It's normal for couples to have contentious differences. It's even normal for couples embroiled in contentious difficulties to ask for help. But to ask for help and ignore it? We find that odd.

© 2018 Erik Douglas Johnson   Schismogenesis

114   One of the joys of lasting, intimate relationships is the fun of pleasing your partner. But if you refuse to be pleased, keep moving the bar, and are chronically joyless, your partner will give up. Let 'em know what makes you happy.

115 Co-dependents are unwilling to let others feel the pinch of their misbehaviors, sacrifice their own well-being for the well-being of others, and are people-pleasers. Separate kindness from enabling, caring from rescuing, and love from safety.

116 A house full of peace and quiet may be boring, but it's a great place to grow, heal, raise kids, recharge our emotional batteries, foster creativity, serve others, gain character, feel safe, have fun, cook, sleep, and eat! So why all the chaos?

© 2018 Erik Douglas Johnson   Schismogenesis

117 Distancers need to stop erecting walls and learn to be intimate. Your partner may not be a dangerous parasite who wants to drain you dry. The more you withdraw, the more they pursue, So stop hiding and negotiate boundaries.

118 It's hard for an overly suspicious partner to trust their mate; they're often prone to find evidence of impropriety that isn't conclusive. What would it take for a suspected partner to earn your trust? What are the facts? What is conjecture?

© 2018 Erik Douglas Johnson   Schismogenesis

119 Many married individuals want mercy from God for their marital misbehavior, but God's judgment on their partners' for *their* marital misbehaviors. That sounds like a double-standard. We can't have it both ways in an equal marriage.

© 2018 Erik Douglas Johnson   Schismogenesis

120 Where is your "*on/off*" switch for happiness? If it's in your partner, look out. You'll be like a marionette on the end of their string. Your mood will fluctuate according to forces outside your control. Learn to be happy from within.

121   If you and your partner enjoy such debates, go for it. But if there are tasks to accomplish, decisions to be made, projects to tackle, and kids to raise, somebody's got to break out of this vicious cycle and ask, *"What do you need?"*

122 *"If you really loved me…"* is a terrible thing to say. Your partner may have 101 reasons why they don't want to do the thing you ask, and they still love you. The phrase is provocative, testy, and smarmy. Find another way to ask for help.

© 2018 Erik Douglas Johnson   Schismogenesis

123　Rarely does your partners dream up ways to aggravate you. Well, most of the time, anyway. Your actions trigger them and their actions trigger you. Who started it? Who knows? Who can end it? You. Stop rocking the boat.

© 2018 Erik Douglas Johnson   Schismogenesis

124 If you lack desire, see a doctor. If you fear intimacy, see a therapist. If you're punishing your mate, deal with anger. If you fear failure, build you self esteem. If your mate is withholding, have a mediated crucial conversation.

125   We sometimes marry a person from whom we believe we'll get what we didn't get from our parents. This puts our partner in a terrible bind, since they aren't our parent. Do not dump unresolved childhood issues on your mate.

126 Demanding sex when your partner isn't in the mood is like force feeding a person. The result is sexual bulimia. Weak marriages aren't improved with unbridled sexual expression. Curbing insatiable sexual appetites improves marriage.

© 2018 Erik Douglas Johnson   Schismogenesis

127 This common marital conflict is often a subconscious ploy to get from our spouse what we never got from our parent: love, influence, attention, safety, or value. But it's a no-win situation since even the best "*re-enactment*" fails.

© 2018 Erik Douglas Johnson   Schismogenesis

It bears repeating. When in a fight with your partner don't call each other names, stick to one topic, work on self-control not spouse control, and take breaks to calm down. And please, don't do it in front of the kids.

FURTHER RESOURCES

Want additional help decreasing relational and emotional stress? Check out our website and store at **www.ErikDouglasJohnson.com.** There you'll find dozens of find free handouts, inexpensive e-books, and moderately-priced hard copy books (all purchased through Amazon.com).

We've developed a series of informational wheels which address marriage conflict (as well as fear, worry, and regret). Adjust the wheel and adjust your attitude by learning positive affirmations. Exchange negative thoughts with positive ones and learn to manage emotions, actions, and habits in response to 16 different situations per wheel (8 per side). The brilliance of cognitive therapy is blended with ancient Hebrew wisdom (Proverbs) into an easy to use therapeutic tool. Give your life a positive turn!

Made in the USA
San Bernardino, CA
24 April 2018